Songs Of Sandy

Poetry Concerning Hurricane Sandy and Other Natural Disasters

Bards Initiative

Editors

James P. Wagner (Ishwa)

Nick Hale

Associate Editor

J R Turek

Cover Art:

Vincent (VinVulpis) Brancato

Songs Of Sandy

Copyright © 2012 by Bards Initiative

All rights reserved. No part of this book may be reproduced or transmitted in any form or by any means without written permission of the authors.

www.localgemspoetrypress.com

Thank you to all those who contributed to this project and to everyone who gave their money, time, and possessions to help those affected by Hurricane Sandy.

Thank you to everyone who spread the word about this book during the extremely short submission period, particularly George Wallace, Ann Howells, Steven T. Licardi and as always J R Turek.

Special thanks to our cover artist Vincent (VinVulpis) Brancato for putting the artwork together so quickly.

This volume is dedicated to all those who were affected by Hurricane Sandy and to all those who stepped up to make life a little easier for them in the midst of destruction.

Foreword

In October 2012, Hurricane Sandy ravaged the East Coast of the United States as well as Cuba, Haiti, and other Caribbean islands. Many people were left without power, heat, or shelter. In some cases, people lost everything.

In the days following the storm, people reacted in a variety of different ways. Some went into survival mode, doing what they could to defend their homes and possessions. Some took advantage of the chaos, looting powerless houses. Still others stepped up to help those who had lost more than just power. Volunteers brought food, clothing, and other supplies to those who suffered most from the storm.

Songs of Sandy is the Bards Initiative's and the Long Island poetry community's response to Hurricane Sandy. On behalf of all of us at the Bards Initiative, I hope that these poems and the money we raise will, in some small way, offer comfort to those who have lost something as a result of the storm. The poems contained in this volume speak of the destruction of the storm and the resulting hardships, but they also speak of hope and recovery.

Perhaps the most exciting and heartwarming thing about working on *Songs of Sandy* was the sheer volume of responses we got in such a short period of time. For me, it was a reminder that no matter what life throws at you, it's possible to recover with help and that when we collaborate to help each other, our potential grows exponentially.

~Nick Hale
Vice President, Bards Initiative

Table of Contents

A Brief Introduction 1

Sharon Anderson 3

    I Will Not Fall 3

David H. Arnsten 5

    Prelude to Wind 5

John A. Brennan 7

    The Storm 7

Elizabeth Jane Brenner 9

    Home 9

Paula Camacho 11

    The Day After 11

Dolores Cinquemani 13

    Christmas Hope 13

Kate Boning Dickson 15

    from the edge of wreckage 15

Peter V. Dugan 17

    The Wake Of The Flood 17

Jessica Goody 19

The Tempest	19
Geraldine Green	21
No Place	21
Nick Hale	23
Contrast and Proportion	23
Mankh (Walter E. Harris III)	25
Hurri-ku Sequence	25
George Held	29
No Time	29
Ngoma Hill	31
Maybe Sandy is another name for Karma	31
Ann Howells	33
Furies	33
Maria Iliou	35
Storm Sandy	35
Vicki Iorio	37
The Surge for Sandy	37
Karen Jakubowski	39
Why Sandy?	39
Denise Kolanovic	41

The Wrath of Sandy 41

Samantha Larosa 43

Small crimes 43

Ellen Lawrence 45

Untitled 45

Linda Lerner 47

The Storm 47

Steve Levy 49

A Power No LIPA can Supply 49

Steven T. Licardi 53

The Year Halloween Was Cancelled 53

Paula Lietz 55

Sandy's Wake 55

Annmarie Lockhart 57

Permanence 57

Chosen Lyric 59

Untitled 59

Gene McParland 61

Rainbows 61

Roberta McQueen 63

The Giving Spirit 63

Barbara Novak 65

The Poet, Stilled 65

Carl Palmer 67

Found in Translation 67

Jillian Roath 69

Halloween Sandy 69

Marc Rosen 71

Untitled 71

Robert J. Savino 73

Feather in the Wind 73

Jen Siebert 75

Resilience 75

Doreen (Dd.) Spungin 81

Einstein's Theory of Relativity 81

as seen through the eyes of a survivor 81

Ed Stever 83

A Letter To Edgar And Emily 83

Julia Thalen 85

Exposed 85

J R Turek 87

After Math, After Science, After Sandy 87

Lauren Tursellino 89

To Reinvest With Dignity 89

James P. Wagner (Ishwa) 91

Me and Sandy 91

Pamela M. Wagner 95

Suffering Sandy 95

George Wallace 97

Beer And Sausages Go Better 97

Samantha Weiner 99

sandy 99

Laura Wysolmierki 101

More Princesses 101

Sally Banks Zakariya 103

Typhoon 103

Ed Zanheiser 105

Debriefing Post-Election And Hurricane Sandy 105

A Brief Introduction

The idea for this book came from the notion that every poet out there with a pen was probably writing down their reflections, thoughts, and feelings about Sandy. I was writing a poem myself when I realized that other people were probably doing the same thing. Once I had power back, I contacted Nick Hale and his enthusiasm for the idea of a special chapbook about Sandy poems matched mine so we immediately threw up a website that was a little rough around the edges to start taking submissions.

The call for this book went out about 2 days after the worst of the storm hit NY and NJ. A little over two weeks later it was filled with submissions from over 40 poets. That's more than we were expecting in such a short timeframe. So *Songs Of Sandy* went from a proposed chapbook to a full anthology.

The poetry in this book is heartfelt, moving, powerful, angry, sad, courageous, generous, hopeful, and reflects in my opinion the entire spectrum of human emotions from stories of selfishness to pure selflessness, reflective of both sides of the human coin, and since most of the poets in here are from the NY, NJ, Connecticut area, some of the places that Sandy hit hard, these are poems right from the heart of the damage.

Thank you everyone who contributed to the book; you have recorded the real emotions during a time of turmoil. And thank you, readers; this book is for you.

~James P. Wagner (Ishwa)
President, Bards Initiative

Sharon Anderson

I Will Not Fall

There were times when my walls echoed laughter,
the clink of glasses,
the murmur of conversation.

There were days when tiny feet
clattered on the stairs,
slid down the halls.

Sunlight sparkled on my windows,
flowers breeze-waltzed in my garden--
a giant elm stood sentinel beside my gate.

But then, terror came;
a demon of destruction
disguised in screaming wind and rushing water.

Elm sentinel flailed and writhed in anguish,
a frightening dance-macabre...
the garden waltzers lay silent,
buried forever in a muddy mass grave.

Now cobwebs rule. My halls stand empty;
echoing only sadness, and the skitter of mice.
This tiny bit of heaven, where laughter sang
      and love abounded,
has been visited by the demons of Hell, yet has survived.

There will again be days when sunlight
sparkles through my windows,
glancing off china, reflecting in mirrors,
marking its passage in comforting warmth.

There will again be flowers in my garden--
the strength of my foundation guarantees it.

David H. Arnsten

Prelude to Wind

I heard the notes
quietly searching, little man listened
to the shingles rustle
eyes down on the old piano
finding melodies
ascending, descending and back again
playing to chase the storm away
I watched television with the sound off
listening to his sweet cacophony, a
serenade to the live footage of dunes washing away
music for the bending of trees
and tumbling lawn furniture, untethered
the despair of starting over
will wait until first light
in the meanwhile
a lullaby from small fingers
in nearly three quarter time

John A. Brennan

The Storm

We were expecting her unwelcome visit thanks to the ingenious invention of Radar, developed during the dark, frightening years of World War II. All we could do was prepare for her inevitable onslaught. She was conceived and born on the African continent and like all newly born, she was small, but would soon grow into an uncontrollable, raging demon.

She knew that she would be well-fed as she wafted slowly out over the rugged coastline and started her journey of utter destruction. She met several others just like herself as she travelled westward, all from the same nursery. Soon they joined together in their deadly dance and began their feeding frenzy. The ocean temperature being warmer than normal became a vast, sustaining hotplate and she delighted in this.

The suction created by her rotating winds allowed her to draw copious amounts of moisture into her ravenous coils and encouraged her to spin furiously. As she approached the Leeward Islands she knew that a useless name and meaningless numbers would be assigned to her in a futile attempt to understand her. Maybe it was believed that in doing so it might lessen her fury but she knew better. She had become a grotesque, howling monster and desired to enter the history books.

She was the first of many more to come and now there would be no stopping her. Sated, she headed straight for the nearest land mass to wreak her vengeance.

Elizabeth Jane Brenner

Home

A sandy spray
A sandy wash
A sandy hope begets a rough start
A ground is murky of sticks and stones
And it's never broken and neither is a home
A home is love
A home is heart
A home has warmth from those around-those are
    where homes start and live for centuries and
    continue strong
Of straw or bricks
Or wood or stone.
With one or a thousand
Hope and love makes a place a home
Which can be carried no matter where you are
just remember home is where the heart is
And hearts will never fall

Paula Camacho

The Day After

D batteries stand like soldiers
while LED lanterns, flashlights,
candles crowd the coffee table,

while yellow and orange snakes
of generator cords drape over
chair and floor. Turned into a war

room of readiness, our living room
lingers in a disarray of unused
and unneeded. The storm barking

around us does not bite, water
bypasses us on its way to the Brooklyn-
Battery tunnel and 86th Street

station. Our trees kick off a branch
or two while the electric gods keep
our lights on and I am thankful

to be spared amid the destruction
and damage of this storm.
Our unused generator given to a son

to save a friend's tank of pet fish
a small gesture, the beginning
of many needed.

Dolores Cinquemani

Christmas Hope

High water and sand
Pushed upon the land
Caused by Sandy's wind and rain
Our hearts feel deeply
All the loss and pain

Like the bridges that connect each borough
Linked like diamond bracelets
Strong and bright, sturdy in heart
We carry over dark waters
The reflected light and hope of Christmas

Kate Boning Dickson

from the edge of wreckage

when things creep back to normal
we will flip on all the light switches
as we enter dark rooms
we will boil water for simple pleasures
of tea or pasta
we will greet neighbors
casually

somewhere close to ordinary
we'll create small zones of comfort
warm socks warm feet
slowly beating back damage
we'll make little places
again feel neat
patches of raked grass
green without smashed
branches and leaves
small sunny spots
without debris

in the proximity of regular
it will be fine
to stop thinking about cold and wet
to focus on insignificance
in a time
when the struggle is less
we will need
to almost remember
and almost forget

Peter V. Dugan

The Wake Of The Flood

Boats from marinas miles away
washed across highways, carried
down Reynolds Channel, swept up
Mill River and Swift Creek
beached on fairways and bunkers
of Bay Park Golf Course.

Further up river at East Rockaway High School,
the newly renovated auditorium
lies in ruins, all seats submerged
except those in the balcony.
The gymnasium floor, its
wood warped, resembles ocean waves,
complete with fish and crabs.

Cars and trucks are immobile,
askew in parking lots and on lawns.
Sink holes erode streets;
branches and uprooted trees block roads,
crush cars and lean on homes.
Television, telephone, internet cable
and power lines torn down,
communication and information cut off
or extremely limited.

Up river and up the road
a woman finds her undamaged hot tub,
still filled with water, standing alone
in the center of Lister Ball Field.

Songs Of Sandy

At night total darkness envelops
the neighborhood, save for the flashlights
and lanterns inside occupied houses.
The smell of low tide, sewage
and burnt gas and oil permeates the air.
The sound of autumn crickets drowned out
by the drone of generators.

The next day, piles of carpet, furniture,
and other remnants and wreckage
form mounds in driveways and on front lawns.
Someone plants the American Flag atop one.
Curbside I find a child's index card
from school, labeled #10 and it reads:

*"Fearing death for himself and the rest of the men,
they decide to build boats and float them down
the Mississippi in hope of finding a Spanish settlement."*

Jessica Goody

The Tempest

Dedicated to the victims of Hurricane Sandy, October 2012

The world has been torn up by its roots.
The huddled masses have been tempest-tossed.
It's like God said, "I'm bored,"
and decided to shake things up.
The day after the world ended,
people looked around in shock and despair:

Buildings ripped as easily as sheets of paper,
debris piled resembling the surface of the moon.
Wooden fences broken like teeth in a fistfight,
the dragon-scales of roof tiles
scattered like shed snakeskin.

All catastrophes are alike; in the aftermath
an Atlantic hurricane is no different
from an Asian tsunami, a jet crash, holocaust, or war.
Chaos and carnage bear the same result,
the same devastation, fear, destruction.

Sherman's flaming siege of Atlanta,
his jackbooted footprints through Southern red-dirt yards.
The regal destruction of the Titanic, a starlit night.
She sits, a dowager decaying gracefully in her
undersea abyss,
shattered porcelain, the salt-stained ivory of piano keys,
and broken heads of china dolls
with one eye socket smashed, the other still blinking.

Songs Of Sandy

The superstitious will say it is an Act of God,
a Biblical plague prophesied,
the come-uppance of stubborn kings.
Animals lie bloated where they have drowned.
Broken glass glitters like ice.
Cars float by like metallic manatees.

The place where I was born has been whirled away,
eaten by the feral ocean.
The Leviathan rose up and howled.
Four generations of my family have lived here.
Familiar streets, the landmarks of my childhood
no longer exist.

Thousands of tree trunks lie tumbled,
yanked from their moorings as easily as lose teeth.
Solid things that one thinks of as permanent,
immobile, eternal as the Rock of Gibraltar
have been uprooted;
homes that have stood for a hundred years or more,
wood, brick and stone reduced to rubble
by the jackhammer of rain
and the banshee's shriek of wind.

Boats lie perched on rooftops. Furniture is shattered
and splintered as if by a brawling giant.
The sleeping serpents of fallen power lines
It is a curse, an apocalypse, an Armageddon.

Geraldine Green

No Place

Another New York City morning
and at breakfast an old man
memories and stories, wrapped
like a small bible, in tissue, snapped
round by an elastic band

"Before you go let me show
you something.

That's Miriam" he told us

and now it's us off to the Hudson
get some fresh air before
meeting a friend for lunch, check out
Hell's Kitchen and all the while I'm

walking the old man's story
married 56 years, never ill, two sons,
both engineers, lived all my life in
Lower Manhattan, now homeless
flooded out, no power, or water
12 floors up, my Miriam.

I saw her, young, dark, curled,
glamorous even and wondered
at their lives together, refugees
from an era of yellow stars
and persecution
mass inflation
barrowloads of paper money

Songs Of Sandy

"It was good here, in America, then ..."

shrugged his shoulders, eyes brown, tired
alive though, as he spoke of this, of that, of
Iraq and Thatcher.

The wind from the Hudson blew
in our faces, as we crossed over
12th, heading for the river.

Nick Hale

Contrast and Proportion

In the days after the hurricane hit,
the Internet was abuzz with
complaints: "I can't take it,
it's so not fair!" "A whole day
without power" "The only way
to I can get online is with my phone,"
"If I go one more day without
T.V, I'm gonna die."
First world
problems flooded my facebook,
and, with a torrent of tweeted
tantrums, nearly drowned out
the other voices:
After the hurricane hit,
the Internet was flooded with stories:
"My cousins lost their homes, and everything
they own,"
people left homeless, jobless and penniless,
going through Book of Job -style suffering
at the hands of the storm.
I also read of the helpful, and the selfless
who gave of themselves in service to strangers.
"Done with work for the day, heading
to Rockaway to hand out food and clothes.
Who wants to come?" Had likes and comments galore.
I read of teachers in Texas
raising a semi truck's worth of supplies
bound for total strangers a 30-hour
drive away.
I read stories of looters

Songs Of Sandy

both looting and being shot,
of chaos and lawlessness
and the death of common courtesy.
It seems as if, the apocalypse has hit
and everyone has gone into "me first" mode
I read hundreds of stories of people
who had just as many reactions.
The way I see it, the storm made some of
us forget what really matters while it
made others of us remember.

Mankh (Walter E. Harris III)

Hurri-ku Sequence

Sandy tells candy-
dates, duct tape your windows &
your mouths, and listen!

winds so strong
that's what
Great Spirit is like

all through the storm
the small stones
stayed with the Earth

sunlight rippling
on computer screen and keyboard
sun's energy

opening the desk drawer
the scissors
works perfectly

note to self:
stop checking
the answering-machine light

note to self:
don't flick
the light switches

 the candle-flame
does not just light
    itself

Songs Of Sandy

cosmic love
something you can have
plenty of

outside the cell-phone store
my first call from . . .
the Crow Nation!

supermarket cafe
free electric juice
charging cell-phone

not just a winter coat,
a winter coat for her
eight-year-old daughter

at the bagel place:
    wacky lady: "you gonna make the toast crunchy?"
    worker lady: "i'm just making toast."
        who needs tv

Marines - Semper Fi
Mankh - simpli fy

after storm quiet --
then the roars
of the generators

no streetlights
the stars
that much closer

without internet
savoring each page-a-day
calendar art

Mankh (Walter E. Harris III)

moon to the west
sun shining through clouds
ripple of breezed leaves

sun's evening rays
on oak leaves, a fiery copper
that can't be mined

why spend money
to go to a Zen retreat,
power outage

sun's light-beings
rippling on the wooden desk —
the real power never goes out

power on
the mellow music station
still mellow

power on
the birds simply
continuing to eat

a neighbor's generator . . .
reminder that some
are still struggling

George Held

No Time

This is no time for poetry,
Sandy's lethal power
And lingering insults
Too strong for sonnets
Or even epic.

No, this is the time
For meditation,
Reassessment,
And just plain worry
About life on Long Island.

How much longer can we
Live on this enchanted isle
While melting glaciers
Raise the water level
And devilish storms

Like Sandy and Athena,
Those violent hags,
Smash up our shores
And leave us powerless
And vulnerable?

How much longer?
How much time?

Ngoma Hill

Maybe Sandy is another name for Karma

some say they should have
named her karma
i'm not sure
if she was a conspiracy theory,
or an act of god
bible thumpers called her
a revelation
a Halloween trick or treat
a politician's opportunity disguised as disaster
some claim it was punishment for sin
but churches were flooded too
steeples and oak trees in the wind
proof that global warming deniers can't ignore
we could say I told you so
and maybe this is a wakeup call
as roller coaster rides are buried in the flood
and marathoners take up hotel space
while many victims have no food
or a place to lay their heads
bodies still being found
in flooded burnt-out homes
with no escape by subways
filled with water like underground cesspools
as Jamie Curtis talks about survival kits on Jay Leno
and tells us to donate money to the Red Cross
yet to show up in Mount Vernon
with gas lines around the block
for gas stations that are empty
meanwhile the major news media
acts as though disaster only happens in america

Songs Of Sandy

as the Dominican Republic, Haiti and Cuba
are ignored by major media
where there is no FEMA to guarantee votes for
    Obama on election day
suddenly we see what it may be like to live in a 3rd
    world country
where lack of gas and electricity is an everyday experience
and half the world is a disaster area
waiting for a relief concert to raise funds
that would not be needed if the wealth was redistributed
and warnings of global warming had been heeded

Ann Howells

Furies

     A cat hunts with quiet equanimity
through shattered rooms.
     Plum blossoms have vanished,
and bluebirds; where are they?
     Everything has been shaken—
dice in a cup,
     tumbled out, harum-scarum,
along the green baize.
     Air gyrated, furled around us,
spindle of frenzied wind:
     tractor-trailers took flight,
transformers became supernovas.
     A total of seventeen tornadoes
CNN announces days later,
     panning brick walls impaled by 2x4s,
wedding dress, pristine, in a field.
     An anchorman enumerates the dead:
surety, security, confidence.

Maria Iliou

Storm Sandy

Listening
Sandy haunting sounds
Penetrating
Crying souls
Stirring winds of
Circle motion
Travels rapidly
Represents of
Lives of deprivation

Deep sorrows of lost,
Lost lives
Houses lost
In debris...fires

Memories restored
In mind, stories
Overjoyed
Wisdom is life experiences

Washed away in deep waters

No objects recall memory
Tears fallen
Lost in shuffle
Sentimental memories
Enjoyment, priceless

Songs Of Sandy

Gloom in your hearts
Wailing cries of
Collected souls
In morning

Blessings
We must move on

Vicki Iorio

The Surge for Sandy

After the surge, a Mary Oliver book I didn't know
I owned floats in my basement.
Its unread contents a bloated blue fish,
my daughter's baby pictures ballerina spinners,
my younger face, an iridescent, swims
with the minnows.

And I hear geese flying away
caring nothing about me
my problems
my loss.

The day after the storm
I watch a seagull gnawing
a T-bone, and I wonder whose dinner that was?
Did the surge reach into a supper window and
        snatch it out?

The second day after the storm
walking in the parking lot
to the FEMA trailer
to the insurance tents
to the Red Cross bus
to the triage

I see the beady eyed seagull gnawing the T-bone,
the bounty of the surge.

Karen Jakubowski

Why Sandy?

Silent voices whisper wisdom
Listen to the stillness
Chaos brings endings
Death of life as we know it
Welcome rebirth
Be released from bondage
Let go to move ahead
Embrace yourself
Open your heart
You are surrounded
By abundant blessings
New life born of flood
Rise like the Kraken
From murky water
Become your own champion
You are a well of strength
Receive healing
Move from selfishness
Become united
Surrender
Renounce the black trail
Shake off the monkey
Swing free from material comforts
Reconnect to spirit
You are whole
Radiate love
Join together
Become a tribe
More than individuals
Together we will be rejuvenated

Share – accept kindness
Shed the snakeskin pride
Release the tethers
Fear chains you
Anger is a rusty shackle
Allow possibility
We are receiving a gift
It falsely appears undesirable
It is not ugly
Shed the wrapping
Hidden within is a fresh start
We are at the dawn of a new beginning
Be a part of the evolution!

Denise Kolanovic

The Wrath of Sandy

The wind was tearing against my home.
Unceasingly, it screeched and moaned
without a moments peace and no phone,
that wind pulled apart my happy home.

For two days prior, we were advised
of power loss and waters rise,
of gas shortages and people's cries
who waited for Sandy's demise.

But Sandy had her own clear sight
and it included a wicked might
that made conflagrations bright
and deluges of waves crested white.

Sandy's a devil, a monster, a hag
who tossed her victims like a paper bag.
Into the darkness soaked to sag
houses fell inward while trees did drag.

We were not ready for her manic and rage,
nor her audacity to enslave us and encage
us without gas or heat or even a wage;
we must patiently wait for the last page.

Samantha Larosa

Small crimes

Nature has her way
Of proving her existence
In unusual ways

There are all sorts of crimes we do to nature
And then she bites back in defense
Is she trying to send us a message?

It still hurts like a fresh cut.
It still causes pain.
I still wish it didn't happen.
But I haven't heard a single person say they'd
      like to change the universe
And actually try to do it.

Ellen Lawrence

Untitled

a long, cold night
trees are swaying
wind gusts blowing
apprehension growing, growing
rain drops splatter
not too bad yet
stormy Sandy not too mad yet
trees are bending
no downpour yet
cannot know what is in store yet
light bulbs flicker
TV sputters
water swishes in the gutters

no more power
pale candlelight
we're in for a long, cold night
morning after
wreckage glaring
neighbors caring, neighbors sharing
no surrender
we will fight
rebuild, restore, banish cold, dark night

Linda Lerner

The Storm

(Oct 28---Nov 2nd, 2012)

the storm didn't stay outside; it entered our streets and yards
uprooted trees smashed through windows and devoured our furniture
the storm still wasn't satisfied

its hunger was insatiable; it frayed nerves and snapped wires
broke into our minds blocking escape routes
thru books and games, stole every kind of light we had

took our breath from us as it poured down our throats
to stop us from talking our way out of it
and flung us away from everything we owned

ripped up memories and played with our minds
unleashed wild animal sounds banging on doors and windows
we took cover with our terrified pets and strangers

and when our mental storm barriers gave we
met in bars cafes and pizza shops to wait it out together
lit up only by flashlights people baked and cooked

prayed to gods we didn't believe in and made
promises about doing better being better
the storm shook the fragile foundations of our existence

we kept on because we didn't know how not to
many were rescued not all; others will be and
homes and businesses restored or rebuilt;

but nobody will make it back to where we once were

Steve Levy

A Power No LIPA can Supply

I sit in the dark and read by candlelight
It's not so bad, thinks I
Humanity has existed without electricity for thousands
 of years
I get to read my book
Something I can't seem to do with the song of TV

We go over to family's house for dinner
They cook up a big meal and put out a beacon, calling
 all mouths
Eat up before it spoils
We talk and share stories
A big crowed eats some of the best food I ever tasted

Long gas lines
Can't believe it's gotten this bad
But a little pre-planning goes a long way
I limit the driving
Carpool with the wife

At night with no heat
We cuddle underneath blankets
Talk of future plans
I almost forget there's no heat
So comfortable we are

On the night of the election
Still without power
This Political Junky goes to the gym for his News fix
Yet the screens are frozen

Songs Of Sandy

A mad dash to the next gym

Along the way
A tanker makes a delivery
With only 10 cars in line
It's like finding gold
In twenty minutes I'm next

Just then
News of Obama's victory over the radio
I'm ecstatic
I share it with the cop next to me
Makes her cold night a little better

I go to pump gas
No wallet
I never bring it with me to the gym
Don't want to lose it
Me, the only dummy on the gas line with no money

I'm so revved up from the election, I can't sleep anyway
Race home to get the wallet
Back on line in another 15 minutes
So are 100 other cars
I wait the hour listening to the sweet commentary

Finally, I hear one voice speak the obvious
If global climate change wasn't plain to see before
Just look at a storm this size, this late in the season
Followed by a nor'easter with the possibility for snow
Let this be a rally cry.

Then the cop looks at me in surprise
Weren't you just here?
I told her my story
She said she would have given me the money
She knew I'd be good for it after only five minutes

Steve Levy

People keep asking me
You got power
I tell them no
They feel sorry for me
I actually don't mind it all that much

Day nine without power
They still ask it
This time I say, Yeah, I got power
No, the electricity's not on
But I got power

Power to overcome the adversity
Power to go on with life
To look on the bright side
We made it out alive
Nothing could be more important

A friend down in Long Beach
Lost his house, everything most would say
Almost everything
He and his family are alive
The things can be rebuilt, replaced

It hurts
It's a big loss
And people without power have a legitimate complaint
All the wasted food and money
But at least we're around to gripe about it.

Most of us, anyway
Let's not forget, many did lose everything from this storm
And it may take months, if not years to recover
Yet through the generosity of each other
We can restore our faith in humanity

Steven T. Licardi

The Year Halloween Was Cancelled

The wind whistled at the exits,
And continued to ring in our anxious ears,
While bulbs sat sighing in their fixtures
And our screens sat inert.
Windows were disemboweled in their frames,
Leaving toothy sockets
In the faces of our homes.
This is what we awoke to.
In spite of all the horror,
Halloween was cancelled.

Flashes of blue light
Illuminated the snuffing darkness,
Wires lying like intestines on the blacktop,
And rivers where there shouldn't be.
Those holes we never wanted filled,
Overflowed.
In spite of all the horror,
Halloween was cancelled.

Apocalyptic sermons filled
The spaces between kin and kinsmen;
Stories of survival told
Over dancing candlelight.
The wind had aided the trees
In exacting their revenge,
Taking men in their driveways
In front of their families,
But it was peacetime.
Splinters of barky skin and limbs
Peppered the crooks of our community.
In spite of all the horror,
Halloween was cancelled.

Songs Of Sandy

We collected evidence of how the sea had shattered
Boardwalks, depositing ships in our flower gardens:
Sea foam peeling back wallpaper
And gobbling up material memories.
One foot more
And maybe we could have saved some things.
Saturated toys osmosed their nostalgia,
While salty brine
Pickled our sorrow.
In spite of all the horror,
Halloween was cancelled.

There was no sweetness to quell
The bitter afterimages.
Waterlogged foundations eroded,
While the ramparts they supported burned above.
We were knee-deep, and still our mouths thirsted.
Mud in our refrigerators
And seaweed on our ceilings.
In spite of all the horror,
Halloween was cancelled.

Radios buzzed with chatter
We would hate any other day,
While books and board games we had neglected
Comforted us.
Children squabbled over
Talks of wasted costumes,
Knuckles biding to knock on doors
And fingers itching to tickle doorbells.
These ghosts will haunt us
In stories yet to be told
And how,
In spite of all the horror,
Halloween was cancelled.

Paula Lietz

Sandy's Wake

her decision making cruel
she had free rein
there on the ocean
she fixated her wrath on land
with too many options
wave upon wave
crashed upon our helplessness
nightmare grit remains
engrained in our minds
her wrath and the aftermath
unfathomable

Annmarie Lockhart

Permanence

hearts carved on pilings
between sand and pier
initials in block letters
forever means for as long
as the boardwalk stands

a moment is permanent
and magic like marker
inscribed on that heart
it will withstand
any angry tide
that surges

Chosen Lyric

Untitled

My name's Brandy
my favorite poet drives a hybrid Camry
29 years old, live on Long Island with my family
in the recession I'm mad at dependence on them: &
they don't understand me
cuz I wanna start my own family
& move in with my boyfriend Stanley
or at least move out, move in with my friend Tammy
but I've been inconvenienced by Hurricane Sandy
it all started when trees fell & I lost power
mad cuz I was watching Kardashians that hour/ then mad
because my iPhone couldn't get service, can't connect
wifi on my iPad
long lines, can't get gas in the car
now I can't joyride in the city, I'm now not allowed
to drive far
so I'm stuck home
no iPhone
almost 30, unemployed and feeling alone
but when it was all over, sandy ruined part of my home
I'm in a shelter, eating canned goods
but my definition of life was misunderstood
I met people whose family members lost lives
who had the courage to stay strong on the inside
I met those who had gas & power the whole time,
& weren't affected
who put in countless hours volunteering, so in town
they were respected
the president sent free gas to Freeport, & went to Jersey,
I suggested
the way he handled Sandy was part of why he was

Songs Of Sandy

re elected
food & clothing drives
at all types of venues gave Americans on the east
coast the fight to not give up & stay alive
it was a time we will remember forever
similar in aura to 911: because in loss, we stood together
I count my blessing as I count sheep, in a shelter pulling
up my covers
cuz we all Held On to hope, showed character, &
Didn't Let Go of one another

Gene McParland

Rainbows

There are no rainbows,
without rain.
There are no victories,
without pain.

Don't start the day with
doubts and fears,
for where they live
Faith disappears.

Keep the Lord in each day.
A smile, a hug, a helping
Hand,
will keep you close to the
heavenly way.

You are loved beyond this
Realm.
So live your dreams,
be safe,
and live under the rainbow
of life.

Roberta McQueen

The Giving Spirit

Spirit, what can I do to help?

Send care packages
of clothing and supplies
send disaster relief
don't forget the toys
for the children for
all hurricane victims
hoping they smile
for just a little while

Adopt a battalion of
soldiers in need
pray they come home
to their families
thank them for their
service and dedication

Spread good will and
cheer to all you meet
it will inspire others
lend a hand when you
can to someone who
will be grateful
to see that there is
light at the end
of the tunnel

Barbara Novak

The Poet, Stilled

9/11
stunned
and grieving words poured
like tears.
Sandy
stunned
and in its post-apocalyptic world
I stand
silenced.

Carl Palmer

Found in Translation

She raises her hand as something is
announced on the radio, motions me
to listen as she turns up the volume.

Being in her country, not at all fluent
in her tongue, no trace of comprehension
as I stare between her and the radio dial.

Turning the volume back down, she repeats
slowly, distinctly the same words heard,
yet still I fail to understand their meaning.

She tunes the dial to an English-speaking
station. Storm surges of Hurricane Sandy
are demolishing America's east coast shore.

Our shock speaks a language we both understand.

Jillian Roath

Halloween Sandy

They said Sandy killed Halloween that year.
That the frights and fun would have to wait until
    2013 rolled around.
Too much damage, people cried.
Too much suffering and misery to even think
Of a holiday.

Well…
I heard eager footsteps that Halloween afternoon.
I heard laughter when only days ago there was nothing
    but cruel wind to listen to.
And I heard the age old cry of "Trick-or-Treat"
    echoing down my street.

So I threw on a black robe and a snarling wolf mask,
Sat down on my porch with the bowl of candy on my lap,
Let my limbs and head hang lifeless.
And I waited…

I waited for the costumed children to come closer
And closer…
  And closer…
    And closer…
Before springing up and roaring as best I could
As they reached for their treats.

And despite all the suffering, lack of power and heat,
Fear of what the next day would bring,
The delighted screams and terrified laughter was
    but a reminder

Songs Of Sandy

Of how resilient we humans are
And how important it was to keep a holiday alive in
      the wake
Of a disaster.

They said Sandy killed Halloween.
From what I could see,
Halloween was alive and well despite Sandy's efforts.
And what's more,
It was fun.

Marc Rosen

Untitled

A woman comes into the FEMA site
Speaks with the staffers,
Then comes into the room I'm in, to the left

A screening room, with comfy seats, the local news on TV,
And most importantly, a giant pile of clothes,
All over the stage up at the front!

We exchange words, and she asks:
"What's all this clothing for?"

A Red Cross volunteer asks if she needs anything
In these times, with a nor'easter approaching,
And the woman herself underdressed for the temperatures,
Warm clothing for her and her daughter is clearly
    called for

The young mother hesitates, stubborn pride telling her
to balk.
She's fine! Save the clothing for someone who
really needs it!
Her protests fall on the deaf ears of her new-found
personal shoppers

Red Cross and FEMA ask about what she'd like,
Tell her how great she'll look in this coat,
Help her fill a giant storage bag
With the yield of her free shopping spree

Tears of joy stream from her eyes

Songs Of Sandy

After enduring silence and indifference from agencies,
her daughter's school, doctors,
She finally laughs; She finally smiles

Clothes damaged in the rains, replaced with new
Needs neglected for lack of shelter and warmth, met
For this family, it won't be as cold a winter as it seemed

Robert J. Savino

Feather in the Wind

There's a place for the perfect poem,
in a perfect storm,
in the library of my home.
Books occupy the perimeter
as they always do,
but there's no green or red lights
of time or connectivity to distract me.
There's no echo from the TV
or hum from the refrigerator.
Outside is cruel, full moon rage,
wind howling, snapping trees into darkness.
What to do? . . . What to do?
Invite the event to a duel
with my feather pen
and ink bottle, in candlelight
and scratch my way to the end
of the page powered by mere sensibility
before its tail spins between its legs
and slowly scurries far away . . . far away.

Jen Siebert

Resilience

There's a storm coming
I heard that one before
It's going to be nothing
Heard that one too
I stand on my front porch
And watch the oncoming wind
Gusts at 20,Gusts at 40,Gusts at 80!
Yeah… right Mr. Weatherman!
I don't see anything yet
A leaf blows across the grass
My neighbor's trash
Floats down the street
Floats because the wind
Is nothing
Nothing yet, I have dressed
The house for your little raindrops
Little breezes
The wood on the windows
Food for me food for the dogs
Food for who knows, Everything closed

Gas is in the back
Packed if we will even need it
For the generator, collecting dust- it must
Still be in the garage Right?

I lift my hands in the air
Open my mouth and breathe my fair share
Of readiness. I arch my back
Let the sound come from the bottom
of my chest
And next… here it comes!

Songs Of Sandy

BRING IT ON!
Bring it on A! B! C!
D! E! Bring it on H! J!
K! L! Bring it on all of them!
Bring it on storm-
Whatever your name is
Sandy, Andrew, Gloria

And I will not paint your name
On my windows
On my plywood boards
On my Ford, On my accord
Because you will never NEVER
Take me!

The storm is coming
What's it again? The name?
Am I going insane?
I guess it's not worth the headache
The strain
To reclaim its name
From my memory
And a tree falls The tree falls
Whose car Is that? BOOM! Jump!
That was some BIG oak tree
And you know, I never thought
THAT one would go down
Maybe the one twisted in the sidewalk next door
Or the dead one by the corner
And I stand on the porch, still screaming
Bring it on!
Bring it on Sandy!
Bring it on Andrew!
Bring it on X, Y, and Z!
Bring it on!
I clench the porch railing with my fists
And the mist
Of rain sprinkles my hair
The twist the twister
Really? Here?

Jen Siebert

Winds getting faster
Faster
FASTER
Wow, That's pretty damn
F A   S   T!
Branches fall and fly into the yard
Siding comes off the houses!
WOAH Screams my boy
Get back! Back inside!
Wires fly like spiderwebs
That were just ripped off the stick
SO THIS, This, This
is what a STORM feels like
I grab the railing banister and close my eyes
The wind dries Them
And the rain soaks them again
All in an instant
Until my skin is red and raw
Bring it on!

White knuckling the wheel
Police come down our block
Our block?
Surely not us?
Why do we have to evacuate?
Nothing bad ever happens here
Right?
We are told leave
Before things get real
Real bad. What is real?
What is real bad? NO
Let's stay here
When do we ever get a real storm?
SNAP! Wires back! Wires snap
Watch out!
There goes the power In the dark
Probably for just a few hours
We had no idea it would be a week
Before it came back

Songs Of Sandy

And I would be walking
Yes, walking
A couple blocks away
Just to wash up
Just to do laundry
To find gas
On a five hour line
Behind two hundred cars
And I don't want to lose my spot
Should have packed more food
I hope my phone battery lasts
Cause that is all we have
That is all We Have
The roof blew off the house
Trees broke the windows
And my car is smashed
The gas Line is N e v e r Moving!
Do you have power?
No, do you? No
Bring it on…
Bring it on…….
Monopoly nights
Playing cards with a flashlight
I never dreamed this might
Be the way we have to live
Not in this life
Yeah, we were hit hard
The dog still barks At the squirrel though
Amazing That little squirrel
The one that always runs into the street
Gets only halfway across
And then runs back (stupid squirrel)
Is really staring at me like my boss
When I am caught on my phone
And I toss It Into the drawer
Really little squirrel?
With your furry little tail?
You stare at me
From half of what was once my fence
With a little acorn in your little mouth

Jen Siebert

Really little squirrel? REALLY?
Since when did the street
Become the beach? Or a salt water river?
Whose boat is that? And HOW
Did that get in my driveway? On her lawn?
Since when Did that house get there?
Where is my car?
Could it have been blown that far?
How did seaweed Get wrapped around the fire hydrant?
Since when do I step down the street
And his house is under three feet of water?
Whose cat is that
Sitting on that floating-
I didn't know we had a boat!
Honey, what is that? Around the corner
Is that a bird Sitting on the stop sign
In that lake?

Was that there before?

Well storm You certainly heard me
You brought it
You brought wind and rain
Flooding and pain
Twisters and twisted curbs, Everything
Everything is in the street
Everywhere it's not supposed to be

And you know what storm
You have not Defeated me
Because I am resilient
WE Are resilient
And we will Get back on our feet
We will rebuild And we will be ready
For next time

We
Are
resilient

Doreen (Dd.) Spungin

Einstein's Theory of Relativity
as seen through the eyes of a survivor

How much water did your basement/car/furniture take?
Oh, not bad. At least we had food.
The lights went out and the heat.
Grateful that Mom didn't live to suffer this.

What I learned about myself
I can survive with less
Goodbye, possessions
Hello, space

Down the street, piles of memories
And necessities
Ruined photos that stab the heart
News of death

How much do you need to continue?
The planets still orbit
The sun has been seen through a heft of clouds
What is safety in the eye of a storm?

What is lost is yesterday's security
What is found is strength for tomorrow.

Ed Stever

A Letter To Edgar And Emily

Not much of a Halloween this year.
Most of the horror
was in the weather,
the aftermath of Hurricane Sandy,
limbs hanging on wires
like attempted escapees
at Dachau or Auschwitz,
tremendous trees laid low
from the folly of their heights.
Slabs of sidewalks ripped up
by roots, yet intact,
an ungrounded perpendicularity,
as if the dead had risen
from their tombs,
and water rushing everywhere,
like deadly lava,
from oceans, bays,
rivers, tributaries,
all seeking dry ground.
Wind and water
howl up a feather of a boy
and plant him in dark soil.
Sailors at sea
surrender memory
along with flapping sails
and the feathered fowl
is sent airborne
without passport
or prior written consent.

Songs Of Sandy

What horrors here, Edgar
that you might have exhumed from
beneath the floorboards?
No wind, no loss of limb,
no Fortunato, no Amontillado.

And you Emily,
at your window,
what horrors did you see
from your safe home,
aside from the funerals
in your brain?
All ink.
No blood.

Let me assure you,
that horror resides
not in imagination
but in reality,
and here comes the wind,
and here comes the water.
If only LIPA were not far behind.

Julia Thalen

Exposed

While around us trees fell crippling
        Lines and strangling communication,
Warmth and comfort, nothing was as it seemed.
        We were exposed.
Winds howled and dismembered
        With merciless precision on our island.
Once again the weather reflected the tumult of
        The secrecy of our love.

As if a novella's plot unfurled up our
        Front steps we learned
That the crucial moment was upon us. We were
        About to meet our climax.
This was no apex of pleasure, but a peak of
        Tension to test our strength
Is our love true enough to withstand Sandy? Will our
        Hands be clasped or reaching?

After the storm surges recessed and the moon
        Waned shame-facedly blanched
Daylight caressed the nature-littered ground. Sinews of
        Hope snapped under tall fallen soldiers
Gawkers drove curiously, away from powerless hearths
        To see the damage for themselves
And we, to our surprise, lay silent. Our prayers
        Answered. We did, indeed, endure.

J R Turek

After Math, After Science, After Sandy

Who knew how vast a Long Island sky could be
    until seen at night without a lit lightpole in sight
so dark, the fallen trees go unnoticed
    so too, the power lines…

Halloween screams on despite the hazards…

Schools closed a week, 10 days
    remain closed around the critical importance
of Election Day voting…
so will kids learn so much more in class in July?

If 7 days equals a week, and LIPA charges too much
per kilowatt hour – and we pay it –
shouldn't the lights be on within days?

What part of evacuate don't you understand?

Is there anything noisier than a post-Sandy generator…
    or more disheartening than power on the next block
and you're still in the dark…

Are there building specs for cell towers, or
    are they really made of playing cards?

Do you think the Joneses are impressed
with your beachfront property now?
Bet the water views aren't the same for you…

Sandy, a Category 1… what would we do in a 5?

Songs Of Sandy

Global warming, less shade from torn-up trees
        but ahh, summer is coming...
Sleety Nor'easter hailing in this afternoon...

If the tankers are full and here
        why are there two-mile lines for gas stations
enclosed in yellow caution tape?

Buy stock in candles and D batteries...

We're surprised, and we shouldn't wonder...
        we do live on an island...

Yet the shelters are open, communities responding
        thousands of anonymous acts of kindness
touching millions of lives to outpower any storm...

Lauren Tursellino

To Reinvest With Dignity

A shadow sets its blood in white and pall
And underneath our shade nothing removes
The amber crusted and retiring moon.
We all retire and yet emerging,
Emerge without our expiring cusp,
Secure the dawn but expire the snake
Afraid of course its fangs do guard our blood.
Lay down my laurels; I revoke their thorns!
I want a crown of green upon my head
And not with light green flesh re-grown in you
But fresh in its womb, your indigo breathe
From there expiring and dead dark green,
Then who will see its death in crusts of shells?
Their jagged rooms within shapely edges
Entombing windows of rock and sea glass.
Whether I am a grain or manifold
I weather your weeds with expiring walls
Who crumble outward inside my bowel
To shovel inward what your surge expends.
I do not wear laurels or thorns or weeds
My colors shift inside lonely prisms-
And sometimes the moon develops tears
To launder over my inhaling surface
To cover it with a trail of mirrors
Who exhale the glaze of suspended ice-
I cannot find my flesh or skeleton
And what can dawn or dusk give me of ghost?
I gave all my blood to take it away
From you and the walls that you dismember
By letting me inhabit you. Forgive.

Songs Of Sandy

Forgive that I am not a mirror,
And can't give you the loss of another grace,
Than what you make from what you'll never see.
That I destroy your flesh, hover its grave,
And without your tears, with my foam suspend:
All I can ever give of grief is here.
Yet you take me when I am calm, or blind
And even thrashing your very bowel,
Make spondees of my tidal deceptions.
Swim within my sad brine, my covered currents,
And covet nothing nor coffin my moon
When it makes surges that revoke our love.
Don't take from me waxing severance
Even as you, expiring the snake,
Forgive the dawn and moon their distant house,
And cannot ever deny my presence,
Make me the ghost that I want to retrieve
To revisit you and remind your blood
Within the house we still haunt together
We're both ghosts tethered to ragged edges.
But I'll remainder you with a smoother edge.
As shadow will always remain its blood,
And hide an amber and retired moon,
Because there's something waned conserving white:
I live my curse when I un-watch your grave
And your grave watches our unguarded house.
You retreat forever and yet you haunt,
And I expire to outlive the snake.

James P. Wagner (Ishwa)

Me and Sandy

After reinforcing
the doors and windows
and everything else around the house
we waited for the storm.
We had no need for the hunt
The emergency supply hunt panic
as our house was well stocked
—almost too stocked
well before her name was ever spoken.
As the rain picked up and the wind got more intense
I spent the first night in my basement, finishing
work on the internet
watching ye old episodes of the Mighty Morphing
Power Rangers
on DVD
relishing the power while it was still there.
Attempting to prepare to be separated from it indefinitely.

Flashlights, walky talkies,
stack of books to my right,
I was set to lose power.
And we did—like we expected to.
I spent the first half hour writing a poem,
Before long,
I jumped onto my manual exercise bike
and started reading chapter after chapter of
the Game of Thrones series to candlelight.
"This isn't so bad, nice to have a break
from all that noise online." I thought
as I started playing old fashioned Pokemon

Songs Of Sandy

on my battery powered Gameboy advanced
(which isn't so advanced anymore, but still fun.)
I went to bed around midnight
After 5 or 6 hours with no power.
When I woke up the next day around 9 in the morning,
the lights were on, the television, the internet,
everything had been restored to me
as if it went on a brief vacation.

For me, personally, the hurricane
was a mere inconvenience.
But for others...
for friends and family members
and fellow human beings
it was much, much
worse.

Houses washed away
Family treasures lost
Flooding up the streets, no power
no food, no rescue for the injured
for untold amounts of time in some cases.
Dozens dead—and this, just in the US
As the media vastly overlooks the devastation
in the other parts of the world.
And as I see the images of the houses under water,
the homes collapsed
the people whose lives
have been turned upside down
by mother nature,
I also see the newsfeed on facebook
Where people my age are complaining
about being without power for an hour
and how "miserable" this makes their lives.

I wonder if any of them realize
that for thousands of years

James P. Wagner (Ishwa)

we had no power
I wonder if any of them realize
that millions and millions in this world today
still live without those luxuries
I wonder if any of them
could put themselves into the shoes
of those who had lost
so much
and I wondered if any of them
even had the foresight
or the wisdom
to even bother
to try.

Pamela M. Wagner

Suffering Sandy

She blew through with a passion of wind, rain and floods
on her mind.
She didn't mean to cause all the trouble
That she did.
She was determined to go through several states and downs
All she could find
She did what hurricanes are meant to do
That was her job description
She changed the lives of everyone that heard her name
Sandy, Sandy, Sandy.
Like a siren in the wind
She unfortunately called to us
All

George Wallace

Beer And Sausages Go Better

beer and sausages go better when you're waiting for
hurricane sandy to come and it's twelve o'clock Monday
morning below pearl street and men in hard hats are
pouring cement under the watchful eye of an urban
archaeologist wearing a fluorescent yellow flacjacket
carrying a clipboard & shooing away a couple of pigeons
-- a plane passes between skyscrapers but the
archaeologist is paying attention to the construction crew
which is ankle deep in a slurry of cement after having
shot straight down a chute and into a steaming pool at
their feet -- they are hard at it too, a shovel man
in suspenders, dude like springsteen with a red bandana
spreading it all out with the flat end of a rake -- they are
in a hurry because the storm is coming soon they need to
knock off work and now here comes a smoothing man
with his bristlebroom, his job is to make those seams
         disappear.
up at the campus the business majors are memorizing
malthus for their one oclock and i know this street will be
underwater soon the east river will come up the
streetlights will go down when night comes it won't be
safe out unless you're one of the gangbangers which I
am not but this too shall pass the river will go away the
lights will come back on morning will return too and men
in hard hats to re-set pearl street with cobblestones for
european tourists in safari coats to walk on, not to
mention mid-westerners in idiotic t-shirts and high heeled
women and men in business suits -- but for now it's just
this crew of men in hard hats and me with mustard on
my hands and a bottle of beer between my knees -- that

and a storm named sandy churning up the coast like a cement mixer full of piss and vinegar ready to steal this pale peaceful October new york city morning away.

Samantha Weiner

sandy

allow me to set the scene
full moon tide
a category one
and a nor'easter
moving up the east coast
destructive weather
changing the landscape
of three states

wind-whipped seas
bringing sand into towns
making them beaches
at one's front door
powerful gusts of wind
snapping age-old trees like toothpicks
and bringing down electric lines
lightning from transformers exploding
descending us into utter darkness
like a scene from a horror film

now drenched in darkness
wrapped in cold
hearing horror stories on the radio
little or no information from authorities
no repair trucks
and a COO
playing with people's minds
while watching them suffer

gas lines stretching for miles

Songs Of Sandy

and some of us only have half a tank
restaurants filled to the gills
because we all had to empty
out our refrigerators and
are in need of a hot meal
libraries used as places for people
to tell and compare stories and
charge cell phones

houses gone
lives out on the sidewalks
lives put on hold

no more coney island
no more asbury park
beaches destroyed
we can rebuild
but we cannot recreate photos
and memories of what was

to some extent
all we have is what was.

Laura Wysolmierki

More Princesses

Where were you when the tree fell on my house?
Where were you when I was cold?
Where were you October 29th?
When the storm came and she was bold?
I have seen so many pictures
So much destruction, water everywhere
In my mind's eye, the seas cascading
As I listened to descriptions on my battery radio
Politicians made speeches and they tried to comfort
As we tried to make sense of this natural nightmare
And we came together as a community
Bringing light, bringing shelter
Bringing food, bringing gifts
As we waited with our chainsaws and our flashlights
Trying to make sense of why this occurred
As we pray and reflect we have no answers
But we are strong and know we will persevere
Because we are survivors we will never lose faith
And life will go on even when death is around us
And more princesses will come to my door next Halloween

Sally Banks Zakariya

Typhoon

Sleepwalking on the lava beach, barefoot on the sharp
black rock, you stared sightlessly at the looming waves,
entranced asleep in those days as you were awake
by the sea and the creatures who live under it.

Read me the ocean book, you'd say at bedtime, pointing
out giant squid and angler fish, neon jellyfish and coral,
that improbable living rock. On sunny days, you'd put on
fins and goggles and join the fish, swimming underwater

like you were born to it, at home like your father
in the sea. But that night, when we led you gently
back to bed, a storm was roiling in the west, remember?
The Pacific was a battleground of wind and water.

It seemed the ocean would reclaim the island
and drown it in the depths it rose from—proof of the
hard truth that not everything endures. Next day
we picked through sodden wreckage, weeping.

It was as though an arbitrary hand had rolled huge
coral boulders through the house, driving splinters
of the bed where you had slept into a jacaranda tree,
dangling a
       crystal vase
  unbroken
          playfully
              in the
                    branches.

Ed Zanheiser

Debriefing Post-Election And Hurricane Sandy

A group of leopards is called a "leap."
So is most political discourse that isn't
a pole vault. The truth walks a tightrope
across the Grand Canyon wishing it hadn't
forgotten the balance pole. It tumbles over
Niagara Falls in a barrel as it wishes for
a space capsule. If a politician met truth
on the street, they wouldn't recognize each
other. Kissing each other's babies would be
like leaning forward into a stiff wind that stops
on a dime. Even ABC's Diane Sawyer felt the need
to stand in the wind and rain on the Jersey Shore
with her wet hair streaked just to let you know
she can exist outside your living room lightbox.
Most preachers' visions of Heaven and Hell
come from John Milton's poetry not the Bible.
Not that they've read Milton. They just sermonize
based on rumors. The Bible was mostly written
by Hebrews who didn't have a heaven or hell
until they bumped cultures with the hungover
remains of the wisdom that was ancient Greece.
To shout from the rooftop "The Bible is literal truth"
is not to defend God but rationalistic materialism
so that God still fits inside your safe deposit box.
Compassion is not to clip your bond coupons as
you watch world hunger on TV and say "Tut, Tut."
It's the altruism that evolved your neo-cortex
so you can shout-down the reptiles in your brain's
basement. And what makes you so sure I know
that a group of leopards is called a "leap"?

About the Authors

Sharon Anderson is a native of Maine, but has lived on LI since her marriage in 1963. She is a published poet actively involved with several writing groups in her area, and is a member of the Advisory Board for the Nassau County Poet Laureate Society (NCPLS).

Dave Arntsen is a LI lawyer, musician and poet. Born in the Bronx and raised in Coram, Dave lives in Manorville with his wife, Doreen, and their five children. He has been writing songs, poetry and prose for as long as he can remember. He is also currently playing in a three piece original band, the lo fi 3, which released its first full length album in 2010.

John A. Brennan was born in Crossmaglen, County Armagh, Ireland, and now lives in Garden City, LI. He writes short stories, poetry and is finishing a memoir. In his writings, he strives to include a lesson and some historical fact. Currently, he's compiling a series of tribute poems to honor musicians who died at age 27.

Elizabeth Jane Brenner is lifelong LI resident and knows firsthand the destruction Sandy caused and is thrilled to be able aid in any way possible. Elizabeth attends Stony Brook Univ and won first-place in a national play writing competition. The author of *There's More to The Story,* this is her third anthology publication. www.ElizabethJaneBrenner.com

Paula Camacho moderates the Farmingdale Poetry Group and teaches poetry in adult education. She is President of the NCPL. www.nassaucountypoetlaureatesociety.com She has published two books, *Hidden Between Branches, Choice* and two chapbooks. She holds degrees in Nursing and Theology and lives on LI with her family.

Dolores Cinquemani is a retired teacher, has been writing seriously for close to five years, with poems published in *Great South Bay Magazine; Creations;* and *Paws, Claws, Wings and Things.*

Kate Boning Dickson has two children, Carrie and Andrew, with her husband Barry. During the weeks following Sandy, without electricity, they all stayed sort-of warm by boiling water on the gas stove and moving pots around the house. When the power came on, they danced, flipping switches, randomly leaving on lights. They are thinking of all those who still don't have lights to turn on.

Peter V. Dugan was born and raised on LI and is a graduate of The New School in NYC. He has published four collections of poetry, edited the *Writing Outside The Lines* anthology, and hosts readings at the Oceanside Library. Publications include *Reckless Writing: The Modernization of Poetry by Emerging Writers of the 21st Century; LI Sounds; Bards Annual; Toward Forgiveness; Asbestos; Good Liar;* and *Road Poet.*

Dr. Geraldine Green is a freelance creative writing tutor, mentor, and visiting lecturer at The Univ of Cumbria. Her collections are *The Skin* and *Passio, Poems of a Mole Catcher's Daughter,* and *The Other Side of the Bridge. Salt Road* will be published summer 2013. Her poetry has been anthologized in the UK, US, and Italy and translated into Greek, German, and Romanian. Geraldine is a frequent US performer. She's an Associate Editor of Poetry Bay.

Nick Hale, like James P. Wagner, was very passionate about working on *Songs Of Sandy*. He is a performance poet, comedian, entrepreneur, aspiring web designer, freelance educator, speaker, and editor. He has a BA in English and an MEd in Secondary Education. Nick has worked on several other anthologies with and helps to manage Local Gems Poetry Press. He is a founder and the current VP of the Bards Initiative. Nick is a literal and metaphorical hat collector, enjoys games, learning new things, traveling, and sleeping. Nick loves comedy of all kinds but has a soft spot for puns and other types of wordplay.

Walter E. Harris III (Mankh) is a writer, small press publisher, and Turtle Islander, and author/editor of numerous books including the anthology *The (Un)Occupy Movement: Autonomy of Consciousness, Practical Solutions, Human Equality* - prose & poetry. He teaches haiku, brush calligraphy, and balancing East-West. He recently started the Holistic Literary Agency. www.allbook-books.com

George Held a six-time Pushcart nominee, publishes widely online and in print, and Garrison Keillor has featured his work on NPR. Held's most recent books, both 2011, are *AFTER Shakespeare: Selected Sonnets* and a children's book, *Neighbors*, illustrated by Joung Un Kim.

Ngoma Hill is a performance poet, multi-instrumentalist, singer/songwriter, and paradigm shifter, who for over 40 years has used culture as a tool to raise socio-political and spiritual consciousness through work that encourages critical thought.

Ann Howells serves on the board of Dallas Poets Community, a 501(c)3 non-profit and has edited its journal, *Illya's Honey,* for fourteen years. Her chapbooks are *Black Crow in Flight* and *The Rosebud Diaries*. She has been nominated twice for a Pushcart and twice for a Best of the Net. Her work has recently appeared in *Borderlands*, *Calyx*, *Crannog* (Ire), *Magma* (UK), *RiverSedge,* and *Third Wednesday*

Maria Iliou is an autistic artist, poet, actress, director, producer, advocate, and host. Maria's been published in *Perspectives, Bards Annual 2011,* and *Rhyme and PUNishment.* Maria is host for

Athena Autistic Artist, which airs on public access tv and hosts the radio show, Mind Stream The Movement of Poetry and Music.

Vicki Iorio, a writer from LI was in the basement when the surge came. She is still trying to shake off that Stephen King experience.

Karen Jakubowski is a native New Yorker who is making a lifelong dream of writing her reality. Her poetry has been published/forthcoming on *Houseboat, Poetry Breakfast, Vox Poetica, The Barefoot Review, First Literary Review-East, Reckless Writing 2012, Spark,* and *Poetry Bay.* Her poem, *A Woman's Intuition,* won the June 2012 Goodreads.com contest.

Denise Kolanovic is a poet and English teacher, published in anthologies and literary journals nationally, and the author of *Asphalt Sounds.* She is active in poetry associations in NY and is a past president/officer of All Cities Branch of National League of American Pen Women. She has organized teen poetry contests and workshops through the Brooklyn Poetry Circle and NLAPW.

Samantha LaRosa enjoys creating things. She is a singer-songwriter who writes lyrics, short stories, and poetry. She currently studies psychology at Stony Brook University and plays shows around NY. She has a lot of heart and hopes that many people find solace in her artistic endeavors.

Ellen Lawrence was born in Switzerland during WWII. An animal welfare worker and retired business owner, she wrote her first poem at ten and has been writing ever since. Her poems focus on her family, her pets and her one-year-old great grandson, Ryan. Publications include *For Loving Precious Beast, Bards Annual, PPA Literary Review,* and many Taproot Journals. She is currently working on her memoirs.

Linda Lerner was born and educated in NYC. Her most recent publication is *Takes Guts & Years Sometimes.* Previous collections include *Something Is Burning In Brooklyn, Living In Dangerous Times,* and *City Woman.* She's been nominated twice for a pushcart prize.

Steven T. Licardi (aka The Sven-Bo!) is a life-long resident of LI and is currently pursuing a BA in Psychology & Philosophy from Stony Brook Univ. At an early age, Steven was diagnosed with a Pervasive Developmental Disorder (PDD); poetry provided him with a way to express himself emotionally. To date, Steven has written hundreds of poems, short stories, and novellas, and is working on his first novel.

Paula Lietz is a widely published writer, photographer, and illustrator who lives in Manitoba, Canada. Publications include *Naugatuck River Review, MaINtENaNT: Journal of Contemporary Dada Writing & Art #4,5,6, Enchanting Verses International Poetry Journal, Voices & Verses, In the Company of Women, Sunrise from Blue Thunder, Rolling Thunder, Twizted Tungz,* and *Red Fez.*

Annmarie Lockhart is the founding editor of vox poetica, an online literary salon dedicated to bringing poetry into the everyday, and the founder of unbound CONTENT, an independent press for a boundless age. A lifelong resident of Bergen County, NJ, she lives, writes, and works two miles east of the hospital where she was born. You can read her words at many fine journals in print and online.

Chosen Lyric is back home in Coram, NY from a year in Port St Lucie, FL and is new to the LI poetry scene. He is the Official Poet of Team Lady Red, a Co-Administrator of Free Poets Collective, and Director of the NY Collaborating Literary Icons under

Rite By Me Studios. He specializes in Spoken Word, storytelling, and metaphors, and strives to release his own book, host his own events, and launch a clothing line.

Gene McParland (North Babylon) is a graduate from Queens College in NY. He has always had a passion for poetry and the messages it can convey. Publications include *California Quarterly, Poets Corner, Poetry Motel, Great South Bay Magazine,* and *Creations.* Like most Long Islanders he was impacted by Sandy and prays for those who suffered so much destruction.

Roberta McQueen is an award-winning poet and teacher, who has hosted poetry groups at the Ashram in Amityville and at local cafes and bookstores. She lives with her husband and 3 companion cats, Prince, Tara, and Sammy.

Barbara Novack, Writer-in-Residence and professor of English at Molloy College, founded and hosts Poetry Events and Author Afternoons and, off-campus, offers creative writing workshops and programs. She is listed in *Directory of American Poets and Fiction Writers* and in *Who's Who* and *Who's Who of American Women.*

Jillian Roath is an undergraduate at Dowling College, pursuing her BA in Creative Writing and hopes to attain her Masters in Library Sciences. Jillian is an active member of Fanfiction.net, and is currently at work on her own novel. She was one of the founding editors of *Conspiracy*, a genre fiction magazine at Dowling College and recently edited *Paws, Claws, Wings and Things,* a pet anthology through Local Gems Poetry Press. She will be editing other poetry anthologies in the near future.

Marc Rosen is Treasurer/Co-Founder of The Bards Initiative who also serves on the NYS Independent Living Council, and was invited to assist FEMA and NYS agencies at a FEMA Disaster Recovery Center sites on LI as a disability consultant. In addition, he has compiled and submitted a report to the Governor's Office on the various ways in which disabled New Yorkers were let down or harmed in this time of need, complete with concrete proposals to address those issues.

Robert J. Savino is a native LI poet, widely published in print and online. He is the winner of the 2008 Oberon Poetry Prize. Robert's first collection, *Inside a Turtle Shell*, is a diverse journey of paths crossed, family and friends . . . lost and found.

Jennifer Siebert is a full time student at Dowling College with a dual major-biology and special education, with a minor in visual arts. In addition, she is editing several of her full-length books. She has been published in several poetry anthologies, including *Perspectives: Poetry Concerning Autism and Other Disabilities.*

Ed Stever is an award-winning poet, playwright, actor, and director, who has published two collections of poetry, *Transparency* and *Propulsion*. He is the current Suffolk County Poet Laureate (2011-13), and poet-in-residence and board member at the Long Island Poetry Archival-Arts Center in Patchogue, NY. He is an Asst Professor of English at Suffolk County Community College.

Julia Thalen is a 25-year old Long Islander who draws inspiration from Classic British poetry, from her family experiences, and from all things nautical. She is studying to teach English. Her current projects include a compilation of her own poems spanning the past decade. While she isn't writing or teaching, Julia spends time travelling always looking forward to the next inspiration.

J R (Judy) Turek is in her 16th year as Moderator of the Farmingdale Creative Writing Group, a Pushcart nominee, and is a widely published award-winning poet. She is an editor, poet, workshop leader, former Executive VP of the NCPLS, Board Member for TNSPS and PRP, Associate Editor and Advisory

Board member for The Bards Initiative, host for PPA, co-editor (with Gail Goldstein) of *Whispers and Shouts: An Anthology of Poetry by Women of Long Island* published by Local Gems Press, and author of *They Come And They Go*. She's a poem-a-dayer. J R, sometimes referred to as the Purple Poet, is a lifelong Long Islander who resides in East Meadow with her soul-mate husband, her dogs, and her extraordinarily extensive shoe collection. msjevus@optonline.net.

Lauren Tursellino has an MA in English Literature from Stony Brook Univ, adores art in any capacity, and is working on her first poetry book, *Persephone*. Publications include *The Abiko Annual, The North Shoreian, College Bound Magazine, Ragazine, The North Shore Sun,* and *The Improper Hamptonian*. Since 19, she has been coping with Systemic Lupus, which has given her an enduring empathy that even exceeds her poems.

James P. Wagner (Ishwa) came up with the idea for *Songs Of Sandy* to give poets an outlet for their feelings about the storm and so the poetry community could do its part for the relief effort. He is the founder of Local Gems Poetry Press and has been editor on several anthologies. James is the senior-founder and President of the Bards Initiative and serves on the advisory board for the NCPLS. James is an award-winning fiction writer, essayist, martial artist, and actor. He also maintains a website and a blog: www.makemoneywriting21.com to help authors find ways to make more money with their writing. His next book will be entitled *The Customer Is Often Wrong*. He would like to thank Nick Hale and J R Turek for their help with putting this book together so fast.

Pamela M. Wagner lives with her husband and son. A nurse, managing a doctor's office, she has been in the medical field for over 30 years and a member of ARE for 30 years as well. She enjoys writing and poetry as well as cooking, traveling, and rescuing animals.

George Wallace is 2011-12 Writer-in-Residence at the Walt Whitman Birthplace, and was Suffolk County's first poet laureate, 2003-2005. Author of 21 collections of poetry, he teaches writing and literature at Pace University in Manhattan, and in writing workshops worldwide.

Laura Wysolmierski is a NYS employee who has been writing poetry for the last several years. Her credits include *PPA Literary Review, Toward Forgiveness, Perspectives: Poetry Concerning Autism and other Disabilities Volumes 1* and *2*, as well as *Rhyme and PUNishment: Comedic Verse.*

Sally Zakariya, a former magazine editor, is a freelance writer and editor. She has studied publication design and turned out self-published illustrated alphabet books on food, literature, and anatomy. Her collection of poems, *Arithmetic and other verses from late in life,* was published in 2011. She lives and writes in Arlington, Virginia.

Ed Zanheiser contributed the poem "Debriefing Post-Election And Hurricane Sandy" to this anthology.

Local Gems Poetry Press is a small Long Island based poetry press dedicated to spreading poetry through performance and the written word. Local Gems believes that poetry is the voice of the people, and believes that poetry can be used to make a difference.

Local Gems is the sister-organization of the Bards Initiative.

www.localgemspoetrypress.com

Made in the USA
Charleston, SC
30 December 2012